HEALTHY NOT CUTE WATER

INSPIRING AND MOTIVATING QUOTES vol 2

FRAZIER CUNNINGHAM

HEALTHY NOT CUTE WATER

PREFACE

This book of quotes is the second in a series that was a labor of love dreamed up during the Covid-19 pandemic of 2020. While 2021 is marginally better than 2020, it is still fraught with the type of worry and fear that Americans haven't faced in generations. Unemployment rates remain high. There are workforce and supply chain shortages. Homelessness, depression and drug abuse are at an all time high. As with the first book, released in 2020, the world needs positivity now more than ever.

Words are powerful. A simple word said at the right time can awaken emotions and propel people into action. Words can be a catalyst for change. While words are not mystically able to solve all of the worlds problems, they can comfort us, move us, encourage us and challenge us.

This book of quotes is compiled with original motivational, inspirational quotes that have been shared with the Healthy Not Cute Water social media community. It is our hope that this book will resonate with you and have positive impact on your life.

INTRODUCTION

Healthy Not Cute Water is a lifestyle brand dedicated to encouraging people to embrace themselves and find the beauty in our differences rather than desperately trying to conform to societies preconceived notions. Our unique stories, backgrounds and personalities is what makes us great! We want to create an environment where people are free to be the best version of themselves. The healthiest version of themselves... mentally, physically, and emotionally.

What Does Healthy Not Cute Water Mean?

HEALTHY: Mind Body & Soul
NOT CUTE: F*ck society standards...do you!
WATER: Like water we have the power to create or destroy. What will you do with your power?

What Does The Healthy Not Cute Water Logo Stand For?

Our Healthy Not Cute Duck is a spin on the story of the ugly duckling. In the classic children's story, a swan's egg accidently rolls into a duck's nest. The young swan grew up unhappy, believing that he was ugly & a misfit because he looked and behaved differently than all the other ducks around him. He was bullied and abused because he was different than the others. When the duckling matured he realized that he was a swan. He was the most beautiful swan of all.

At the core of the story is the fact that the ugly duckling was unhappy, not because there was anything wrong with him, but because he was trying to be something and someone that he wasn't. There was true beauty inside the ugly duckling just waiting to get out. Once he accepted himself for who he was he found a place for himself in a pond full of swans where he was free to be the best version of himself. Our Healthy Not Cute Duck is the embodiment of this story. The duck is not the prettiest duck we have ever seen and yet he has confidence and self-assurance. He is meant a portrait of an individual that may not always fit in, or comes from somewhere different than the majority, but is still able to not only succeed but thrive!

The word water is used in our name as a metaphor for life, strength and resilience. Much like the ugly duckling there is more to water than its appearance. Water is soft and flexible and yet it can be hard and rigid. Water can either create or destroy. When water encounters an obstacle it finds a way around it or through it. Water will bend but it will not yield. Water can be still and yet still run deep. We should all endeavor to be like water.

"EVERYONE IS BORN WITH SONG IN THEIR HEART. ONLY THE BRAVE WILL SING"

W hen you look at someone that is successful do you ever wonder how they got to be who and what they are? I'm talking about people who have done things so big that they have changed the world – like Jeff Bezos.

What makes these people so different can be summed up in one word – Bravery. Jeff Bezos was brave enough to follow a dream that most thought was impossible. The internet was new and shiny when Jeff Bezos began a web business delivering mail in his garage. He believed that the Internet would change everything and could be his vehicle to success. This was during a time when most people thought that the internet was a passing fade and home computers were only a thing for the rich. None of the naysayers deterred Jeff Bezos though. He was brave enough to stick with it. Even when bills were overdue and people lost faith in him and look at Jeff now. He is the richest man in the world. Read that again –

BECAUSE JEFF BEZOS WAS BRAVE WHEN OTHERS WERE AFAID HE IS NOW THE RICHEST MAN IN THE WORLD.

Are you ready to be brave?

PRAY TO GOD -> NOW USE THE TOOLS HE GAVE YOU

YOU DON'T HAVE TO BE THE BEST TO BE EXTRAORDINARY

YOU ARE A STAR SO START SHINING!

"IF YOU DON'T SACRAFICE FOR YOUR DREAMS YOUR DREAMS WILL BE SACRAFICED!"

"Y ou gotta give up something to get something" - this is the rule of life. How about, "Nothing in life is free" or "Nothing worth doin' is easy." All of these quips are conveying one universal truth: A life worth living isn't easy. That dream you have deep down in your soul, that one thing that excites you, that gift from God, that requires attention. It's not something you do when you get to it. It isn't something that you do a few minutes a day. It is something that you make time for. You have to sacrifice something on the alter of success if you want to see your goals realized. John Hanna, CEO of Fairchild Group shared how he sacrificed one year when he was trying to build his business and money was scarce ('The Business Insider' April 8, 2017.)

"My wife and I couldn't afford to pay rent, so we decided that she

would stay at her sister's while I stayed at my mother's. We didn't leave each other; we just lived apart until I got back on my feet."

Keep in mind that John had a young son at the time. He was willing to sacrifice a year out of his families life so that he could provide a much greater life for them later.

"Recently, my son (now 25) confronted me about leaving them for a year. I explained that it was necessary to build the business and give him the life he deserved. My son works with me today and is reaping the rewards. It wasn't an easy pill to swallow at the time, but I knew the sacrifice would eventually be worth it. Today, money isn't a problem. And it's because I did what had to be done in order to keep building my dream."

OPPORTUNITY IS LIKE CROSSING A BRIDGE THAT LOOKS LIKE IT'S ABOUT TO FALL BUT LEADS TO A POT OF GOLD. EVERYONE S SCARED TO CROSS IT UNTIL THEY SEE THE FIRST PERSON DO IT. ONLY THEN IS EVERYONE ELSE READY TO CROSS BUT THE BRIDGE CAN'T HOLD THE WEIGHT OF THE CROWD AND FALLS APART.

FIGHT FOR WHAT'S IMPORTANT TO YOU! NEVER SETTLE FOR LESS THAN YOU DESERVE!

DREAMS ARE DANGEROUS FOR PEOPLE STUCK IN THE STRUGGLE. STEP OUT OF YOUR BOX AND IMAGINE A NEW REALITY.

THINK
OUTSIDE
THE
BOX

"YOU GOTTA THINK OUT OF THE BOX IF YOU WANT TO GET OUT OF THE BOX RESULTS"

Have you ever had a problem that no matter which way you turned it over in your head you just couldn't seem to solve? Have you ever shared the issue with someone and found that the solution was something that you never would have though of? Was the other person a genius or were simply missing the solution because you were stuck in a box, a mode of thinking, and the solution was just out of reach?

I know that I have found myself in this position numerous times but when I am able to step outside of what is comfortable, leave my little box, a world of possiblities magically opens up for me.

YOU CAN LEARN TO BE OR NOT TO BE

NEW PERSPECTIVES OPENS THE DOOR TO NEW POSSIBILITIES!

AS IN SPACE, THERE IS NO UP OR DOWN - IN LIFE THERE IS NO EASY OR HARD WAY. IT'S ALL PERSPECTIVE.

BIG ADVICE FOR ANYONE
DOING ANYTHING -
DON'T WORRY ABOUT IF
YOU ARE RIGHT OR
WRONG... JUST DO IT.

"BIG ADVICE FOR ANYONE DOING ANYTHING - DON'T WORRY ABOUT IF YOU ARE RIGHT OR WRONG... JUST DO IT."

In the pursuit of any endeavor, one of the most paralyzing fears is the dread of making a mistake, of veering off the path that leads to 'right.' This apprehension can stunt growth, creativity, and even happiness. But here's the big advice for anyone doing anything: Don't worry about whether you're right or wrong. Just do it. Action is a great teacher; it offers lessons that contemplation simply can't provide. Every stumble, every detour, every 'wrong' decision is an opportunity for growth, a stepping stone to becoming a more resilient, insightful, and adaptable individual. The key is to embrace the uncertainty, the unknown, and sometimes even the mistakes, as these are the experiences that mold you into a better version of yourself. The paralysis of indecision often causes more damage than any 'wrong' action ever could. So, take that leap of faith, and remember—doing something is almost always better than doing nothing.

THE TRAIL IS ONLY HAUNTED IF YOU BELIEVE IN GHOST. MINDSET AND PERSPECTIVE IS EVERYTHING!

WITHOUT DARKNESS THERE IS NO LIGHT. WITHOUT FAILURE THERE IS NO SUCCESS

FACES DON'T LIE.
WORDS DO.

AN OPEN MIND LEADS TO OPEN POCKETS

"MAKING MISTAKES IS THE BEST WAY TO COLLECT DATA. STANDING STILL IS HOW YOU LOSE"

-HEALTHY NOT CUTE WATER

"MAKING MISTAKES IS THE BEST WAY TO COLLECT DATA. STANDING STILL IS HOW YOU LOSE"

L et me clarify, I do not believe in mistakes and I have passed this belief down to my children. There are no mistakes in life, there are only opportunities....an opportunity to improve, and opportunity to learn and an opportunity to do some self-reflections. I can honestly say that I do not regret any decision I have made in my life, good or bad. Each and every decision has brought me to where I am and shaped the person I am today and I happen to think that I am awesome.

Could I have done somethings differently? Yes, absolutely! But do I believe my actions were a mistake? NO. Life has lessons to teach us and I am here to learn. I have earned my strips and I am proud of it.

*NOTHING WRONG
WITH BEING HUMAN,
EXCUSES MAKE FALLING
SHORT A FAILURE*

IGNORANCE IS NOT ONLY BLISS BUT USEFUL TOO! AS BABIES WE LEARN THROUGH CONSISTENT TRIAL AND ERROR. AS WE GET OLDER WE BECOME FEARFUL OF LOSING. DON'T LOSE ALL OF YOUR CHILDHOOD TENDENCIES!

WE FALL TO GET BACK UP

NOTHING IS PERFECT EXCEPT THE
FACT OF BEING IMPERFECT.

-HEALTHY NOT CUTE WATER

"NOTHING IS PERFECT EXCEPT THE FACT OF BEING IMPERFECT"

Perfection is overrated! Why be perfect? Why strive to be perfect? I struggle with perfectionism. I am an "If I can't do it right I won't do it all!" type of person. I used to think that was a positive trait but as I have grown and matured I have realized that it is a detriment. Perfectionism is really just insecurity. What I am saying when I revert to perfectionism is that I am afraid of failure and rejection. I make a million excuses for why I can't do the uncomfortable and convice myself that if it can't be done within my comfort zone then it just isn't worth doing.

This thinking is the kiss of death when you are trying to make progress. Instead of looking for perfect results step outside of your box and just get it done. I have adopted this when cooking. I have learned new cuisines during my time in Covid lock down. My biggest challange was mediterrean food. Gathering the ingredients and the elaborate steps for some of the dishes was a roadblock at first but at some point i decided that I wanted Chicken Ghallaba more than I wanted a perfect meal. I substituted ingredients, simplified the cooking process, skipped the overnight marinade and just went for it. No, it wasn't the same Chicken Ghallaba I would have gotten from La Shish but it was close enough and it was delicious! My Chicken Ghallaba sandwiches are perfectly imperfect and I love them!

YOUR GREATEST SUCCESS IS JUST ON THE OTHER SIDE OF YOUR GREATEST FAILURE

I PREFER FAST NOT PERFECT

*WHEN YOU BUMP
YOUR HEAD ENOUGH
YOU LEARN TO GO
AROUND THE WALL*

"TOMORROWS MEAL COMES FROM TODAYS' VISION"

Stop waiting!!! Do you have a passion, a dream or a vision living inside of you? Do you keep putting it off for another day? Have you ever wondered where you would be if you had pursued your dream?

I have a cousin who was so talented and compassionate and likeable but he could only concentrate on what was right in front of him. He couldn't see that what he was doing in July 2019 was going to be a fatal choice in August.

My dear cousin, my best friend, my ride or die had health issues but it was birthday wish to fly to Las Vegas to see Janet Jackson for his birthday. I begged and pleaded for him to wait. To reschedule his flight but he had eternal optimism. He believed that a weekendf wouldn't do too much damage. He felt ok. He had a clinic to visit while he was in Vegas. He was taking a friend to keep an eye on him. He believed he was all good. I knew the truth though. I knew that his decision could have disasterous results, and it did. The morning of Saturday, August 17th my cousin was in a great mood. He'd went to the concert Friday night and according to him "Janet Jackson looked me dead in the eye. We made a connection!". He sent me pictures and videos of his trips to tourist locations and promised to stop by the M&M store for me later on in the day. Not more than 3 hours after that phone call I received another call telling me that he was gone. His heart had simply stopped beating on the Vegas strip.

His heart had been week for years due to an blood infection from years earlier. At home his doctors knew his history and how to stabalize him but he wasn't so lucky in Vegas. Could his decision to go to Vegas when we knew his health was on shaky ground have led to his premature death? ABOSLUTELY! I believe with all of my heart that if he'd been home that weekend we could have saved him but unfortunately he couldn't see the bigger picture. He couldn't see that *"Tomorrows Meal Comes From Today's Vision."*

TODAY IS A NEW AND BLESSED DAY. WITH THE FAILURES YOU LEARN A PATTERN OF WHAT NOT TODO..AND WHAT WORKS BEST!!!!

- ADA GIBBS

IF TODAY SUCKS GIVE TOMORROW A TRY

*THE EARLY BIRD GETS THE
WORM BUT THE SECOND
MOUSE GETS THE CHEESE!*

"TODAY MIGHT FEEL UNBEARABLE BUT JUST LOOK TO TOMORROW, GOD'S GOT THIS!"

There are days when life feels overwhelmingly bleak, when even the act of getting out of bed seems like a Herculean effort. It's easy to get mired in the here and now, your vision clouded by the weight of current struggles. But it's crucial to remember that each day is but a single chapter in a much larger narrative. On the toughest days, I've found solace in looking beyond the immediate hardships, in focusing on the promise of tomorrow. The belief that God has a plan, even when life seems like an inscrutable maze, has been a beacon of hope for me. "God's got this," I'd tell myself, and suddenly the burdens of today start to feel a little lighter, a little more bearable. This outlook doesn't magically solve all problems, but it offers a momentary reprieve, a breathing space, and sometimes that's all we need to keep going.

EVERY MORNING YOUR DREAMS ARE REBORN ANEW

MONEY IS ONLY AN INSTRUMENT OF WEALTH! CONDUCT A DAMN SYMPHONY

LIVE WELL, PURSUE YOUR GOALS AND BE KIND TO OTHERS

"A DREAM UNEXPLORED IS A GIFT WASTED "

E ach one of us are born with a purpose. Each one of us are meant to bring something into the world. Maybe you have a love of cooking or are good with children. Maybe you have an innate ability to handle money or your presence is soothing to those in need. Whatever you gift may be, don't waste it. The world needs what you have to offer.

IN LIFE WE HAVE A CHOICE - EITHER WAKE UP OR STAY ASLEEP...BUT REMEMBER YOU CAN'T REACH YOUR DREAMS IF YOUR ASLEEP

TRUST THE PROCESS BUT DON'T RUSH IT! ANYONE CAN BE GREAT BUT IT'S NEVER OVERNIGHT

THERE IS AN OLD EXPRESSION MY MOM USED TO USE, "YOU ARE CRYING HUNGRY WITH A LOAF OF BREAD UNDER YOUR ARM." PEOPLE WANT A LOT OF THINGS IN LIFE THAT ARE MORE OBTAINABLE THAN THEY THINK! JUST HAVE CONFIDENCE AND GO FOR IT!

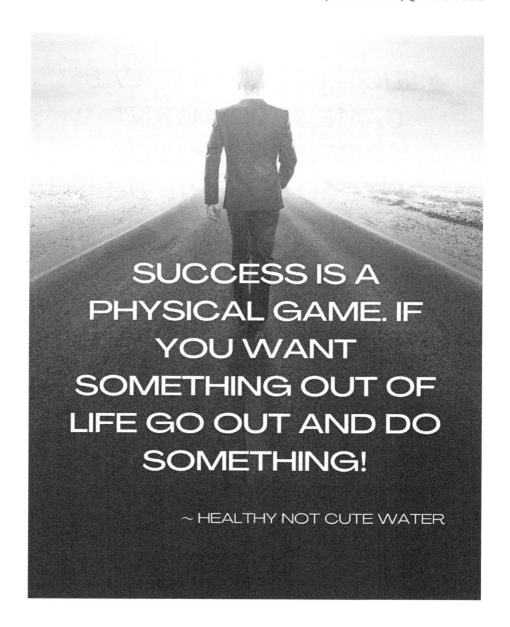

SUCCESS IS A PHYSICAL GAME. IF YOU WANT SOMETHING OUT OF LIFE GO OUT AND DO SOMETHING!

~ HEALTHY NOT CUTE WATER

"SUCCESS IS A PHYSICAL GAME. IF YOU WANT SOMETHING OUT OF LIFE GO OUT AND DO SOMETHING!"

Many people mistakenly believe that success is purely a product of good fortune or intellectual prowess, but the truth is that success is a physical game just as much as it is a mental one. It's about taking tangible, deliberate steps toward your goals, not just daydreaming about them. The difference between those who achieve their aspirations and those who don't often boils down to action. You can have the most brilliant ideas, the most ambitious dreams, but they will remain just that—dreams—unless you go out and do something about them. Sitting back and waiting for opportunities to come your way is like trying to catch fish without casting a line. It's about getting your hands dirty, grappling with challenges, and throwing yourself into the fray. The journey toward success isn't just a cerebral one;

it's a physical endeavor that demands sweat, effort, and an unwavering commitment to doing, not just thinking.

FORWARD THINKING (WHEN YOU WANT SOMETHING) IS NOT FIGURING OUT HOW TO BUY IT BUT FIGURING OUT HOW TO MAKE IT!

REAL SIMPLE MATH: YOU CAN FAIL 100 TIMES BUT IT ONLY TAKES ONE TIME TO BE SUCCESSFUL

IF YOU WANT A HOME RUN YOU SHOULD SWING HARD AT THE BALL. DO MORE AND YOU WILL GET MORE. GO AT LIFE LIKE IT'S YOUR NEXT HARD SWING

STOP THINKING SMALL, IT'S NOT SUSTAINABLE IF YOU WANT MORE IN LIFE!

~ HEALTHY NOT CUTE WATER

"STOP THINKING SMALL, IT'S NOT SUSTAINABLE IF YOU WANT MORE IN LIFE!"

The mantra "Stop Thinking Small, It's Not Sustainable If You Want More In Life!" isn't just a burst of motivation; it's a fundamental truth that many of us often overlook. We sometimes find comfort in setting limitations, constructing a mental safety net that keeps us from falling too far. But the irony is, these self-imposed boundaries become the very ceilings that cap our potential. When you think small, you don't just sell yourself short—you also deprive the world of the greater contributions you could make. Small thinking might offer the illusion of low risk and easy wins, but it's a trap that will keep you tethered to mediocrity. If you have grander aspirations, you need to elevate your thinking. Sustainable success and profound impact don't come from playing it safe; they arise from the audacity to dream big, the courage to break free from self-imposed limitations, and the unyielding will to stride confidently into the expansive terrain of possibility.

THE POSSIBILITIES ARE LIMITLESS IF YOU ARE!

CHASE YOUR DREAMS AND MEET THE PERSON YOU WERE MEANT TO BE

YOUR MIND IS LIKE AN ALL YOU CAN EAT BUFFET. YOU CAN CONSUME AS MUCH HEALTHY THINGS OR UNHEALTHY THINGS AS YOU WANT.

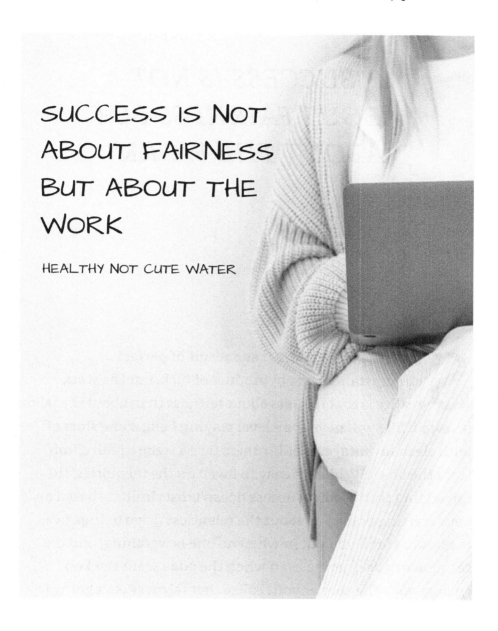

SUCCESS IS NOT ABOUT FAIRNESS BUT ABOUT THE WORK

HEALTHY NOT CUTE WATER

"SUCCESS IS NOT ABOUT FAIRNESS BUT ABOUT THE WORK"

S uccess is often painted as a result of perfect circumstances or a byproduct of luck, but the stark reality is that it is less about fairness than about the labor invested. Life will never be a level playing field; some start off with clear advantages, while others face a steep uphill climb from the onset. While it's easy to dwell on the inequities, the unyielding truth is that success doesn't discriminate based on your starting point. It's about the relentless drive to improve, the hours of toil you put in when no one is watching, and the resilience to keep going even when the odds seem stacked against you. The sooner you realize that fairness isn't going to hand you success on a silver platter, the quicker you can roll up your sleeves and put in the work that will.

*BECOME SUCCESSFUL
BY CONTRACTING TIME
NOT EXPANDING MONEY.
TIME CANNOT BE MADE
BUT MONEY CAN*

LIFE IS LIKE MATHEMATICS, FOR EVERY PROBLEM THERE IS A SOLUTION

KNOWLEDGE HEALS OLD WOUNDS AND PREVENTS NEW ONES

MY MOMMA ALWAYS TOLD
ME THAT NOTHING EASY
IS WORTH DOING.
CHALLENGING YOURSELF
PROMOTES GROWTH

HEALTHY NOT CUTE WATER

"MY MOMMA ALWAYS TOLD ME THAT NOTHING EASY IS WORTH DOING. CHALLENGING YOURSELF PROMOTES GROWTH"

My momma always instilled in me a simple yet profound wisdom: "Nothing easy is worth doing." At first, as a child, I misunderstood, thinking this was an invitation to seek out hardship for its own sake. But as I grew older, I came to realize what she truly meant—growth comes when you step out of your comfort zone. When you take the path of least resistance, you may find temporary relief, but you rob yourself of the invaluable lessons that come from facing and overcoming challenges. It's through tackling the complicated, embracing the difficult, and wrestling with the uncomfortable that we not only discover the extent of our capabilities but also expand them. Momma's words became a guiding mantra, encouraging me to lean into adversity rather than shy away from it. In doing so, I've found that it's in the crucible of challenge that the most meaningful growth occurs.

YOU HAVE THE FIRE WITHIN YOU TO BURN DOWN ALL THE OBSTACLES PUT IN YOUR PATH

DON'T LET SOCIETY DICTATE YOUR WORTH. CHOOSE YOUR OWN PATH, FORGE YOUR OWN WAY. BE HAPPY AND HEALTHY AND UNIQUELY YOU!

POWER IS A VACUUM! EITHER YOU ARE IN CHARGE OR THEY ARE

SOMETIMES A CLOSED MIND ADDS
THE WEIGHT THAT MAKES YOUR GOALS
HARDER TO OBTAIN

HEALTHY NOT CUTE WATER

"SOMETIMES A CLOSED MIND ADDS THE WEIGHT THAT MAKES YOUR GOALS HARDER TO OBTAIN"

A closed mind can often be the heaviest burden you carry on the path to achieving your goals. It's like strapping on a mental backpack filled with stones of prejudice, preconceptions, and stubbornness that only serves to weigh you down. When your mind is closed, you're not just resisting new ideas, you're also blocking out possibilities, solutions, and opportunities that could accelerate your journey toward success. An open mind, on the other hand, is like a vessel waiting to be filled with fresh perspectives, knowledge, and experiences. It allows you to adapt, innovate, and evolve, turning obstacles into stepping stones. So, if you find your goals appearing increasingly elusive, consider unpacking the unnecessary weight of a closed mindset to lighten your load and bring your aspirations within reach.

AHHH, AS HUMANS WE THINK WE ARE SOOOO SMART! THE TRUTH IS THE ONLY REASON HUMANS ARE THE APEX SPECIES IS BECAUSE WE HAVE THE ABILITY TO PREDICT THE FUTURE

*REMOVE ALL OF
THE UNNCESSEARY
DISTRACTIONS SO THAT
YOU CAN FOCUS ON
WHAT REALLY MATTERS*

*IF YOU LIVE YOUR LIFE
DAY TO DAY THEN YOU
ARE HEADED FOR A
SHORT FUTURE*

"VISION + FOCUS = SUCCESS"

T o get work done on schedule, we often find ourselves chasing multiple goals at once – and even thinking about more things to do at the same time. The workload isn't the problem, necessarily. The problem is the idea we have to do it all at once to be successful.

Stop and breathe. Focus on one thing at a time until you complete it. After that, move onto the next thing.

NOTHING STAYS THE SAME! EITHER IT IS GETTING BETTER OR IT IS GETTING WORSE. YOU MAKE THE CHOICE

*LOOKING AT THE
WORLD WONDERING
WHY IT HAS SO MANY
PROBLEMS...IT'S HARD
DOING THE RIGHT THING*

IS BEING BROKE THE EASY WAY OR IS GETTING RICH TOO HARD? - MINDSET DETERMINES BOTH!

CHALLENGE YOUR SELF EVERYDAY. YOUR BIGGEST COMPETITOR IS YOU

- Healthy Not Cute Water

"CHALLENGE YOURSELF EVERY DAY. YOUR BIGGEST COMPETITOR IS YOU!"

D o you know what happens when you sit on your behind for up to 18 hours a day? I do and so does my body. Some really great things came out of my forced isolation during the pandemic. I picked up a few skills, finally made the time to take a few courses I've been putting off and I got to know my kids on a whole different level...but I also picked up snacking, developed a taste for rich foods (I was learning to cook new dishes), and sweet tooth.

Let me tell you, while my mouth enjoyed my new pandemic habits, my waistline definetly did not. When the restrictions were lifted I found myself struggling to shed the pounds. I would often lose motivation because I wanted instant gratification. Other people were getting it together and I found myself with a case of "letting the Joneses get me down". I had to realize that I was not in a competition with my neighbor, cousin, spouse ect...I was only in competition with myself. I have no control of how or when others met their goals. I only had control over my goals. All I could do is try to do better, try to do more, than I had the day before. In truth I was my biggest competitor.

NO MATTER WHAT
THE INDUSTRY AN
ENTREPRENEUR
WILL FIND A WAY

IT DOESN'T MATTER WHO YOUR PRESIDENT IS! REAL FREEDOM COMES FROM INVESTING IN ONES SELF!

THE BEST WAY TO GROW YOUR BUSINESS IS TO 'MINE' YOUR BUSINESS

"THE ENTREPRENUERSHIP JOURNEY STARTS AND ENDS WHENEVER YOU WANT IT TO!"

B eing an entrepreneur is not easy, but it is rewarding. Entrepreneurship is a lifelong journey, and the road is different for everyone. Some Entrepreneurs hit it out of the park almost immediately others work towards entrepreneurship for years before finding success. Some people start their journey right out of highschool, some go to school and get a college degree, others stumble into it later on in life.

Regardless, the journey begins when make the decision to go after your dreams.

*TRY TO PICK THE POSITIVE
OVER NEGATIVE WHEN
IT IS AN OPTION*

GO OUT THERE AND GET THAT F U MONEY! YES, THERE'S AN ABUNDANCE OF MONEY ON THIS PLANET AND IT'S F U (FOR YOU)

MONEY IS ONLY AN INSTRUMENT OF WEALTH! CONDUCT A DAMN SYMPHONY

IF YOU SAY MONEY WON'T MAKE
YOU HAPPY YOU ARE EITHER
LYING OR STUPID!

HEALTHY NOT CUTE WATER

"IF YOU SAY MONEY WON'T MAKE YOU HAPPY YOU ARE EITHER LYING OR STUPID!"

Now wait....I know your probably rolling your eyes and have your lips twisted. You probably don't agree with this statement but hear me out...Can you really be happy with an empty stomach? When you are stressed out about bills? When you can't get the medical attention your child needs? Now let's ask these questions another way...

Will it make you happy to be able to have access to healthy, delicious, filling meals whenever you are hungry? Will it make you happy to have more than enough to pay all of your bills? Will it make you happy to have enough money to be able to protect and care for your children?

....hmmmm I made you think didn't I?

No, money is certainly not the basis for happiness but it goes a long way towards putting you in the position to pursue happiness and grab it with both hands when you find it :-)

*MARKETING IS SMART
PEOPLE TAKING
ADVANTAGE OF
DUMB PEOPLE*

EVEN THE BEST HAVE TO LEARN HOW TO FLY AGAIN. STAY HUMBLE AND BE READY TO FALL AND GET BACK UP

*YOU DON'T HAVE TO
BE SMART TO BE RICH.
YOU JUST HAVE TO
BE DUMB NOT TO.*

IN ORDER TO BE GENEROUS YOU MUST FIRST BE SELFISH AND GET YOURSELF TOGETHER

-HEALTHY NOT CUTE WATER

"IN ORDER TO BE GENEROUS YOU MUST FIRST BE SELFISH AND GET YOURSELF TOGETHER"

S ome people are selfish by nature, just because they put themselves and their needs above all other. Other people are selfish for a purpose. Take the medical student for instance - to successfully get through the grueling schooling and long hours a medical student has to be selfish. They don't have time to hang out with their friends like they used to. Money must go towards books and necessities. They must distance themselves from drama and petty grievances. This is not because they are selfish by nature but because they have a greater purpose. In order to selfless they must be selfish. In order to help humanity by being a healer and a giver they first had to get themselves together.

WORSE THING A POOR PERSON CAN DO IS SPEND MONEY TO LIVE LIKE THEY AIN'T POOR

*DUMB PEOPLE MAKE
SMART PEOPLE RICH*

THINK ABOUT YOUR TRIBE NOT JUST YOURSELF!

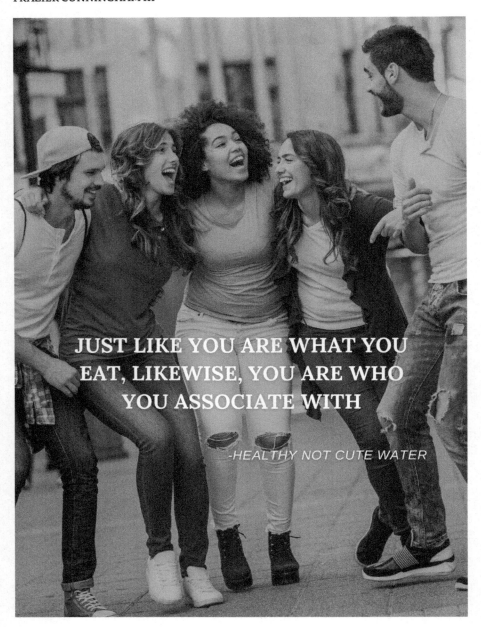

JUST LIKE YOU ARE WHAT YOU EAT, LIKEWISE, YOU ARE WHO YOU ASSOCIATE WITH

-HEALTHY NOT CUTE WATER

"JUST LIKE YOU ARE WHAT YOU EAT, LIKEWISE, YOU ARE WHO YOU ASSOCIATE WITH"

T he Covid-19 pandemic is a life changing event but all of it hasn't been bad. During this time I had the chance to learn new things, find new passions and evaluate my life. I took a long hard look at everything from how I interacted with my family to my choice of friends. Do you know what I found? I found that I could do better on both fronts. My friend circle was almost the same as it had been in highschool and it was comforting. They were all great people but we had went in different directions a long time ago. I have a gene that I inherited from my mother. I call it the "I'm gonna be great" gene. This gene drives me to reach new heights of success, to top myself year after year, to seek out new possibilities.

My friends, a great group one and all, do not share this drive with me. They are content to live in their home town, marry their highschool sweetheart, work at the local factory and never see or try anything new. Now, don't get me wrong, there is absolutely nothing wrong with that but it just isn't for me. Not at all. I was a swan in a pond full of ducks! I realized as much as I loved these people it was time to move on. I needed a new friend circle. One where we could each bring something to the table to help uplift each other. One that I could share my thoughts and goals with. You know the old saying, 'You are the sum of your 5 closest friends'? Well I did the math and realized that I am capable of much more. I made one of the hardest decisions of my adulthood and let most of my friends go. I challange you to look at your circle with an objective eye - are you a swan in a pond full of ducks?

*PEOPLE ARE LIKE PEPPER!
ONLY GOOD IF YOUR*

SELECTIVE ABOUT HOW YOU USE THEM

WHEN YOU TALK TO PEOPLE YOU ARE TALKING TO THEIR REPRESENTATIVE....FOLKS AINT 100!

*JUST BECAUSE YOU
HAVE COMPANY THAT
DOESN'T MEAN THAT
YOU ARE NOT ALONE*

AVOIDING STRESS ISAVOIDING RESULTS

-HEALTHY NOT CUTE WATER

"AVOIDING STRESS IS AVOIDING RESULTS"

We have all been programmed to believe that stress is bad and should be reduced or eradicated from our lives. However, not all stress is bad stress. In fact, stess does provide some benefits -

1. Heightened awareness
2. Improves performance
3. Strengthens immunity (short term)
4. Increases resiliency and motivation

The name of the game shouldn't be avoiding stress and making everything "easy". Instead we should learn to cope with stress appropriately so that we can mitigate the negative side effects and maximize the positive to propel us to success.

I DON'T WANT TO ESCAPE MY REALITY. YOU CAN'T DO THAT HIGH! #SOBERLIFE

IT'S SMART TO QUESTION WHAT'S WRITTEN OR TAUGHT. WHAT IS

DUMB IS TO IGNORE THE TRUTH!

APOLOGIES ARE CHEAP BUT ACTIONS ARE PRICELESS

SOMEONE ELSE'S NEGATIVITY DOES NOT HAVE TO BE YOUR REALITY

-HEALTHY NOT CUTE WATER

SOMEONE ELSE'S NEGATIVITY DOES NOT HAVE TO BE YOUR REALITY

I know you have a person, everyone does, that is just negative all the time. No matter what they just can't seem to be happy. If they see even a sliver of happiness in someone else they feel the need to stomp it out like a roach. Yeah, I have one of those. It's a family memeber so I can't trade up (even though I wish I could). I realized that just because they are miserable I do not have to be miserable too. I can choose to focus on positivity. I can choose to minimize the time that spend with them. I can protect my mental health and there is nothing wrong with that. You do not have to expose yourself to anyones toxic negativity. Put your peace and mental health FIRST!

*MIRROR NEUTRONS
SHOW US HOW WE WILL
BE LIKE THE PEOPLE WE
SURROUND OURSELVES
WITH SO SHY NOT
HANG AROUND WITH
SUCCESSFUL PEOPLE?*

*SELFWORTH HAS
NO PRICE TAG!*

*LIFE IS TOO SHORT
FOR SOME AND TOO
LONG FOR OTHERS*

"WHEN YOU ARE BETTER THAN AVERAGE YOU MUST BE BETTER THAN AVERAGE"

R ight before the Olypmics began I began watching a 21 year old sprinter by the name of Sha'Carri Richardson. She was/is the fastest woman in the United States and brought an excitement and flair to the sport that had been missing since FloJo. I was looking forward to watching her run the relay and 100 meter and then, right when the entire world had their eyes on her and it seemed as if her career was headed to the moon she was disqualified for drug use.

I was floored. What would possess this young girl to throw away everything she'd been working so hard for? As it turns out she turned to marijuana to deal with the death of her mother. She was unaware of the tragedy and was informed by a reporter during an interview and went into an "emotional panic". This was just days before she was set to hit the world stage. Sha'carri admits that she knew the rules about drug use she knows that she shouldn't have broken them. She told a NBC Today Show host "I know what I'm not allowed to do and I still made that decision. [I'm] not making an excuse or looking for any empathy."

The truth is that I *could* empathise with Sha'Carri. She is young and despite her enormous talent she is only human. But what I also know is that old adage "with great power comes great responsibility. Because of her talent and because she was better than average *she had to be better than average.*

STOP LISTENING TO PEOPLE ABOUT MONEY THAT AIN'T GOT NONE

MY MOM USED TO TELL ME ALL THE TIME 'ONE HAND WASHES THE OTHER.' THIS EUPHEMISTIC STATEMENT MEANS THAT WE ALL NEED TO HELP EACH OTHER. COULD YOU IMAGINE IF YOU DIDN'T HAVE BOTH HANDS WASHING EACH OTHER? DIFFICULT!

NECESSITY IS THE PIONEER OF INGENUITY

"I DON'T WORRY ABOUT WHAT I HAVE DONE. I ONLY WONDER WHAT I CAN DO"

John F. Kennedy was the 35th president of the United States. Full of optimism and charm he famously said '...And so, my fellow Americans: Ask not what your country can do for you - ask what you can do for your country." during his inaugural address on January 20, 1961.

The next line is less quoted but just as impactful - *"My fellow citizens of the world: ask not what America will do for you, but what together we can do for the freedom of man."*

The point of his speech was to implore people of all races, nationalities, class, income brackets and backgrounds to unite in the cause of advancing freedom throughout the world.

President Kennedy was looking forward to what could be done

by in the future and what his role would be in that change. Likewise I try to be a forward thinker. I know from experience how very, very, very hard it is not to dwell in the past. To rehash mistakes and wallow in regret but I know that nothing good comes from living in that space. In order to see progress you have to keep moving forward and this is a concept that President Kennedy understood and with those 17 words he motivated a nation. Therefore my mantra is:

"I DON'T WORRY ABOUT WHAT I HAVE DONE. I ONLY WONDER WHAT I CAN DO"

BE WILLING TO GET YOUR ASS KICKED TO BE KNOWN

IN ORDER TO BE CHAMP
YOU GOTTA GET
PUNCHED IN THE FACE

DON'T SAY "I'M TOO OLD", INSTEAD ASK YOURSELF "DO I EVER QUIT?"

WE ALL START OUT THE
SAME BUT IT TAKES LOVE
AND COMPASSION TO END
UP UNIQUELY DIFFERENT

HEALTHY NOT CUTE WATER

"WE ALL START OUT THE SAME BUT IT TAKES LOVE AND COMPASSION TO END UP UNIQUELY DIFFERENT"

While it may seem that we all begin life as blank canvases, the truth is far more nuanced. Each person's journey is shaped by the love and compassion they both give and receive. These transformative forces don't just make us 'better'; they make us uniquely ourselves. Compassion allows us to understand the depths of human experience, while love gives us the courage to express our individuality fearlessly. Over time, these virtues etch indelible marks on our character, making us stand out in a world that often values conformity over uniqueness. While genetics and environment play their roles, it's love and compassion that shape the clay of our being into distinct works of art. So, while we may start with similar raw materials, it's this blend of love and understanding that ensures we end up as unparalleled individuals.

OVERCOMING ANY ADVERSITY TAKES THE RIGHT TEAM/ FAMILY DYNAMIC!

WHAT WILL YOU DO FOR ATTENTION? SHORT OF TURNING WATER INTO WINE LIKE JESUS CHRIST AT THE CANA WEDDING?

*DON'T YOU DARE THINK
FOR ONE MOMENT
THAT GOD WILL EVER
TURN HIS BACK ON US!
WHAT WE NEED NOW
MORE THAN EVER IS
FAITH AND PRAYER.
GOD LIKES HIS PEOPLE
STRONG SO HE TEST US -
THIS TOO SHALL PASS*

YOU CAN'T TELL A BLIND MAN TO CLOSE HIS EYES

AFTERWORD

Ok, now that you have set here and read through all these quotes I hope that they have touched you in some way. I hope I was able to make you mad, make you sad, make you happy and make you think. I hope that these words and stories have not fallen on deaf ears.

It is also my sincerest hope that you will use these words to motivate you to reach new heights, improve relationships, explore new possibilities and find new strength. I know that writing this book has definetly helped me. It was like therapy being able to share my thoughts and stories with you. Who knows, maybe there is another book brewing within me right now....

Thanks for reading!

ABOUT THE AUTHOR

Healthy Not Cute Water (Frazier Cunningham Iii)

Please follow Healthy Not Cute
Water on Socia Media:

https://linktr.ee/
HEALTHYNOTCUTEWATER

Made in the USA
Middletown, DE
01 October 2023

39746870R00086